The Inte
You & Change

A Woman's Empowerment Guide to LEAP to HER Unknown

Lorene,

may the words in this book
challenge your thinking and
leap you beyond where you are
today. Your spirit is electric
and my hope is that you will
Sit in the moments of this
book, reflect, renew and
simply soar with a renewed
spirit!

Lolita E. Walker
July 2019

The Intersection of You & Change

A Woman's Empowerment Guide to LEAP to HER Unknown

LOLITA E. WALKER

2018

First Printing: 2018

ISBN: 978-1-7327928-0-7

Library of Congress Control Number: 2018910922

Published by Lolita E. Walker /
Walker & Walker Enterprises, LLC.

16405 Livingston Road, #804

Accokeek, MD. 20607

https://www.lolitawalker.com

Ordering Information:

Special discounts are available on quantity purchases by corporations, associations, educators, and others. For details, contact the publisher at the above listed address.

U.S. trade bookstores and wholesalers: Please contact Walker & Walker Enterprises, LLC. Tel: (443) 353-9121or email info@lolitawalker.com.

The Dedication

This book is dedicated to SO MANY who have helped me along my journey of continuous change, in particular my daddy, **Emanuel A. Walker.**

While I believe and firmly know that God lends us his children for only a limited time, it is never easy being parted from someone who has been such a stronghold and core foundation of influence, excellence, and drive in your life. My loudest cheerleader, my forever advocate, my harshest critic, my accountability partner before I truly realized what that was, my one-half of a powerful parental pair who always reminded me that God is at my center, my occasional pain-in-the-ass, my go-to for EVERYTHING. He was a self-proclaimed doctor, lawyer, pastor, nutritionist, and president of all organizations, wrapped in one. My SMSgt in the United States Air Force, this is dedicated to my forever role model, no doubt grinning from ear to ear, who affirmed to me as a child that I would be a published author. **So here you are daddy, this is dedicated to you! Thank you for always being you.**

TABLE OF CONTENTS

THE ACKNOWLEDGEMENTS

My acknowledgements run deep for all those who have supported my journey. First, I acknowledge my Heavenly Father and the Lord of my life, **Jesus Christ**, my strength, my encouragement, and my light when occasional darkness overshadows my pathway forward. Your presence, direction, and unconditional love are humbly appreciated and revered. I acknowledge my son, **Walker**, who even at 6 years old, is the epitome of strength, perseverance, love, & living fearlessly free; my mom, **Evelyn L. Walker,** who passionately holds her end of parental support higher each day and continues to be a strong advocate on my entrepreneurial journey; my brother **JD Walker**, a calming presence through miles of separation and an understanding voice, notwithstanding any change he is experiencing; my two living grandma's, **Beatrice Evans and Lucille Walker**, who, at 87 and 88 years of age, are the rocks of my family and whose sacrifices have paved my way; my many aunts, in particular **Aunt Hope and Aunt Joy**, who through their Jamaican roots, carry on what my daddy would if he were here; my DC and VA family, who are too many to name, but hold me in the best and worst of times, in particular my boy and girl wonders, **Ronnie, Byron, Elmora, and Joy,** who double as founders and worker-bees of the PR & Marketing Departments for my business; my "Dine-a-licious Divas," **Qiana**, my ride or die at all times, **LaVonda**, a "sister rock" I lean on often **and Dr. Safiyyah**, who, ever so calmly, talks me off the ledge whenever necessary; my Alpha Delta line sisters of Alpha Kappa Alpha Sorority, Incorporated, namely **Carla, Amata, and Tara**, who are unbreakable support and who have physically been with me through laughs, tears and continued growth; my graduate school professor and mentor, **Dr. Stacy Blake-Beard,** whose organizational leadership class helped me discover "my voice" and whose support for this, my first book, is forever etched in the powerful foreword that awaits you; my Boston "Partnership" sisters, **Denise and Stephanie**, who show up and believe in me, even when I waiver; and **Olayinka**, my corporate partner-in-crime, the first to monetarily invest in my dream of empowering others to embrace, act, and thrive in their greatness; my former husband **Wynndell**, who blessed me with a phenomenal son, amazing lessons, and who is a strong pillar of support to this day; and last but not least, my best friend **Faye**, who is one of the strongest and most focused women I know. Regardless of time, all of our connections remain as vibrant as the day we met. I love and appreciate each of you and could not have traveled this journey of change without your support, encouragement, prayers, and love. I acknowledge each of you as invaluable support leading to the birth of Walker & Walker Enterprises, LLC.

As I embrace the many blessings bestowed upon me, I am rooted in the foundation of two strongholds of change in my life - **my father, last name Walker and son, first name Walker.** I stand at the forefront of our Enterprise. Thank you!

THE FOREWORD

Written by Stacy Blake-Beard, Ph.D., The Deloitte Ellen Gabriel Chair of Women and Leadership and Simmons University School of Business.

....

There is no expected pace for inner learning. What we need to learn comes when we need it, no matter how old or young, no matter how many times we have to start over, no matter how many times we have to learn the same lesson. – Mark Nepo, The Book of Awakening

"*The Intersection of You and Change*" is a gift that may be coming at a perfect time – a time of change and challenging decisions about how you will manage that change. This book is a guide to accompany you as you find your own pace for learning. Lolita Walker's book is an exquisite invitation to manage change in your life by creating your own path. Not just any path but a way forward.

I opened the manuscript of this book with the intention to quickly scan it in preparation to write an informed foreword. From the opening words, I was drawn in by Lolita's candor and the strategic activities that she has provided. I highly recommend this book because I went from reviewing the book to actually using it as a tool to help me navigate my own change. The book evokes several emotional responses -- there were moments when I felt incredible joy and times when I cried. What I most appreciate is that Lolita has written a book that allows you to hold both – the joy/elation and the fear/sadness that accompanies change.

Using the metaphor of a train journey, Lolita invites you to expand your horizons and open up new vistas. The framework for each step in the journey is useful. Each chapter has three parts that are introduced by an acronym, which serves as a foundational poem as you enter each of the stops aboard her change train. Lolita starts with wisdom about navigating the different aspects of change. With each of the three steps, she shares her own experiences, bringing each to life. Finally, Lolita asks informative questions and offers a space for you to assess where you are and what you need to do to be your best self. When you are your best self, there are no limits to what you can do. But as we know, every journey begins with the first step. Reading … no, engaging with this book is a fabulous first step. Enjoy!

THE PREFACE

A deep breath in and a deep breath out is what I did for the second time, as I looked at the clock on the cluttered, yet somehow organized, nightstand beside my bed. The tissue-box my son had converted to a spaceship, the best-selling book I had yet to begin, and the caddy that housed everything from remote controls and pens to miniature toy cars, were all sitting in perfect reach.

With one last twist, I would finally muster up the energy to rise. The thoughts of daily challenges gathered in my mind, as though waiting in line for tickets to the next blockbuster film. The emails, calls, meetings, and projects due by the end of the day, were also vying for number one on the "solve-me-now" list.

These realities were enough to force my eyes back to their resting place and my head deeply within the pillows to my left. A slight turn allowed work emails to help me strategize the day and a calendar scroll reminded me of who I was meeting at work, after work, and post my son's after-school activities.

Whew!!! Not bad for 40 minutes! 3-2-1, let's go! I woke my little guy, got dressed, prayed over our day, and stood in the mirror as he and I verbally declared our affirmations. We were out the door to start our 10-12-hour Walker & Walker routine.

I must confess that as I write this, I feel exhausted, simply from re-experiencing what my normal was for almost two decades. I was numb to the unnecessary stresses mounting atop my shoulders. Does this day-to-day routine sound familiar?

Even if your morning is not as hectic, you too, may run on autopilot from the moment you wake.

Well, hello Ms. Phenomenal Superwoman, who makes magic happen daily and oftentimes hourly. I am Lolita and am so pleased to meet you!

Whether you are a power woman who directs her children's activities, a corporate boss making big impacts, an educator who shapes and develops our youth, or an entrepreneur who launches new ideas, you are in fact a phenomenal woman who deserves to unapologetically be, give, and receive the best of you. Hands down and absolutely! I hope you agree that it's time that you slow down, pause, and simply breathe! Think about it. What would happen if a few of your tasks slipped into the following day? What would really happen? It's time to renew yourself and craft the story you want to actively tell for your life, the story that takes you from where you've been to beyond where you want to go. It's time to navigate through the story that allows you to embrace, act, and thrive in the midst of circumstance.

It's time to renew *you.* You have earned it and you absolutely deserve it! Let's try a quick, intentional breath while focusing on what is happening in and to your body. A deep breath in through your nose of the positivity and serenity that you are allowing into your space at this moment and then a deep and slow breath out through your mouth of the words "can't," "won't," and "maybe" as you allow them to escape. Do you feel your shoulders, your neck, your head, and your mind simply relax? Allow this breath to permeate your body. Consider trying it once more before we begin.

THE INTRODUCTION

There are plenty of books where experts tell you the best way to direct your journey or re-structure your life without understanding you, your prior circumstance, or your future vision.

Well, **THIS IS NOT THAT BOOK!**

Over time, our experiences have been packed, stored, and padlocked with success, fear, and/or uncertainty. The keys to unlock them lay deeply hidden. This book offers you strength to not only grab and unlock those bags, but to also use what's inside to help you embrace your challenges and triumphs, act in your strengths, and thrive in the greatness that lay within YOU!!

This is the book I wish I had.

I invite you to journey this book, as a passenger aboard Lolita's Change Train, where each of the 17 chapters are designed as unique stops along your individual journey. At each new terrain, you'll encounter acronyms of poetry that makes you think, personal stories that are relatable, and short exercises that lead to your self-awareness and discovery.

Your thinking will be challenged, your vulnerabilities surfaced, and limiting beliefs uncovered. You'll leave with increased clarity and action toward what you can control. You'll rediscover your inner you and own how your story will best be crafted. I only ask that you trust the process, which pushes you from your comfort zone and out of your own way. Please do the work at each stop before travelling to the next. When you are ready, simply close your eyes and

LEAP aboard Lolita's Change Train! There is one little reminder, however. To change is an individual choice and to sustain that choice involves support. Whether you want to dust off the "you" before "life" simply happened, sort through thoughts of a promotion, divorce, layoff, new child, or any variation of your status quo, this book reminds you of the affirmation that you are already the greatness you desire.

This book will take you on a journey to ***The Intersection of You and Change.***

THE COMMITMENT

Are you **committed** to hopping aboard this Change Train? I ask because "commitment" is a scary word for some, yet this is where we begin our journey. Let's shake-up the comfort zone and LEAP into YOUR unknown!

My Commitment to You is that I will journey with you! Through this book, we will foster trust, support, actions, and plans that guide your transitions within changing situations. These renewed spaces will allow you to give, receive, and sustain with a clear frame of mind.

Your Commitment to embracing change begins with you!

I ____

(insert your name), on the date of

________________________________, am committed to a journey of freeing my mind to explore new and diverse perspectives. I am open to self-renewal through the exercises in this book and will be accountable for my commitments. I will use my passion, power, and purpose to drive my self-discovery, actions, and intentions.

EMBRACE.

Welcome to the terrain of Embrace.

Embrace is defined as an act of accepting or supporting something willingly or enthusiastically.

The six stops ahead will challenge you to EMBRACE YOU.

Stop 1: Journey Junction

JOURNEY

Journey Junction is the place where all decisions come to be explored

Open your mind, close your eyes, and refer back to your vision board

Unleash your thoughts, your passions, your blocks, and your fears

Remember to affirm your faith and strengths aloud so you continuously hear, that

Now and forever, your journey will be travelled with only a chosen few

Experience the unexpected and allow yourself to start anew

You are power and you are confidence, so trust this journey that is crafted especially for you!

Welcome to Journey Junction!

THE STOP: THE JOURNEY

This stop is about trusting yourself along life's journey to choose which junction you will journey next. It's about remembering you possess strengths that have gotten you this far and knowing these same strengths have so much farther to take you. Your journey is the junction or intersection where your experiences and values meet your choices and decisions. It's where many considerations force you to choose what and who will strengthen you. It's where you take a deep breath, hold on to your faith and values, and walk with your head high, facing forward, despite the difficulties you may anticipate.

MY STORY: MY JOURNEY

I stood there, still and undeterred. I was at "Journey Junction" looking at my crossroads with feelings of excitement, fear, failure, disappointment, and passion. These emotions raced through my body as though I was competing in a track meet. With hands sweaty, yet with a bit of calm, I picked up the phone. It had been 22 years of flying solo, away from the parental nest and 4 years of mom being widowed, living as a retiree. I found myself at a junction in life where I needed to once again seek help. I'd been taught there was absolutely no harm or shame in admitting you were at a crossroads and that possessing the will to ask, is what exemplified strength. I was on a journey of entrepreneurship, soon approaching my one-year anniversary, and there I was, at another one of life's "journey junctions."

I took a breath, said a prayer, dialed her number, and calmed myself knowing that she would not let me fail. Right? Here it goes. "Hello," she answered in a soft tone. "Mommy, I plan to continue my business full-time and reducing costs are a must. I called to ask you to please consider us moving in with you for two years so I can make this dream happen." I listened for a moment and only heard silence. I continued on. "I know I'm on the cusp of something great! I see it, I feel it, I am at the edge of touching it." I paused, yet there was still silence. This time my heart was beating so loudly that I knew she could hear it through the phone. "OK," she finally answered. "Let me think about it and get back to you." "Huh?" I thought, but dared not say. I am positive at this point I was not breathing. My heart instantly sank. This was not the response I was expecting. When the adrenaline slowed down, I realized I was still standing at the same crossroad. I was at the intersection of "Breathe Boulevard" and "Leaping Lane." What options did I have? What could I control? What resources could I leverage to help me forward? Which road would I choose to journey?

YOUR STORY: YOUR JOURNEY

Name an instance where you find yourself at a junction in your own journey?

____

____

____

____

If you were to name the crossroads at your junction, what would they be called?

____

____

____

____

What is the largest fear at your crossroads?

____

____

____

____

What would need to happen for that fear to come true?

____

____

____

____

Now ask yourself, what is in your control? What can you do so those fears don't manifest into reality?

____

____

____

____

The journey to change is NEVER easy!! While we may dream of the greatness that lies ahead, getting there is emotional, uncomfortable, and personal. Besides feeling overwhelmed at times, it is important that you are functioning in a productive space without losing yourself and others in the process.

Consider sharing your journey and articulating it to someone aloud. Consider asking them for specific help to support you at your "Journey Junction."

Stop 2: Transition Turnpike

TRANSITION

Transition Turnpike is a unique journey of its own

Race too quickly or stay too long, you'll come across folks you've previously known

Ask questions, seek guidance, and drive accountability every chance you get

Never say never because you don't know what surprise may be a good fit

Start with the ending, journey to the middle, and finally your renewal will shine a light

Infuse energy, commitment, and patience so your light flickers bright throughout the night

Tell yourself that transition occurs over time, with every inch in the palm of your hands

Intertwine a reminder that you control your actions, because you will and absolutely can

Overwhelming feelings of anxiety and fear will drop by with hopes to stay

Nip it with a boost of faith and confidence, for this transition bridge promises headway

Welcome to Transition Turnpike!

THE STOP: THE TRANSITION

This stop is about owning your period of change. During any transformation, the only thing you have jurisdiction over is how you choose to transition through whatever change you are undergoing. Think about it. Though we oftentimes feel there isn't much we can control, there are still a few things left that are ours. You own the power over your behaviors, your energy, your spirit, your actions and reactions. You own your words. This stop is about being intentional in your movements and making each moment count, knowing you have a specific goal to reach. You are in control of how you get there.

MY STORY: MY TRANSITION

He was gone, yet this new "he" was here and what seemed like everywhere. He was not my dad but was filling a void where my original "he" once was. Why were my actions toward him so curt and uninviting? He seemed to be nice, had done nothing ill-willed, and yet I simply wasn't yet ready to take on anyone new sharing, what I felt was a sacred space with my mom. My dad was gone, she had a boyfriend and, in my mind, it was simply too soon. How dare she move on and attempt to fast forward me to where she was in her journey of a newfound happiness. She was in the renewal phase of her transition bridge and I had not yet gotten through the ending of what originally was. I was stuck in, what felt like quick-sand, yet I was sinking at an even faster pace. She was trying everything she knew to help me navigate, but it was something I needed to do on my own. What were all of these feelings? Why and how was she navigating her transition so quickly, yet I seemed to stay stuck in what once was? How could I navigate my "Transition Bridge" to be the daughter she needed and taught me to be? How could I move on and not lose what I still loved about my dad?

YOUR STORY: YOUR TRANSITION

Modeled in part after William Bridges Transition Model of 1991, I'll use a bridge to represent the three phases of transition. To identify where you are and acknowledge where others may be, this exercise will help you understand and transition through change.

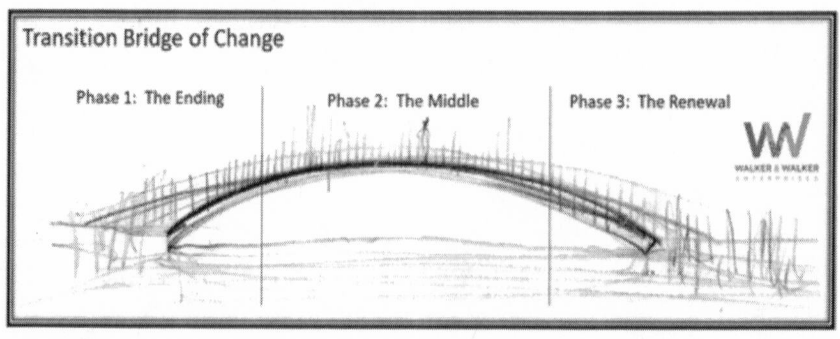

	Phase 1: The Ending	Phase 2: The Middle	Phase 3: The Renewal
The Feelings	Sadness, loss, denial, frustration, them-vs-us mentality, anger	Resentment, confusion, anxiety, impatience, skepticism	Excitement, acceptance, commitment, energy, openness to new beginnings
The Realities	You must accept the ending of something to then accept the newness of another. This is not always easy. The focus on what you can control is helpful in this phase.	You may feel that chaos is all around and that you are always busy. You may be taking on more, see lower morale, or gaps in your normal productivity. Surprisingly, creativity and innovative ways of thinking may be sparked.	You are seeing and feeling a new and revived energy from those who are now embracing change alongside you. You are able to highlight big and small wins of success and results.
The Reminders	Settling in this phase for an extended period may force you to be left behind. It can also mean those who depend on you could adopt your mindset, then struggle with moving to the next phase.	You and/or some who are on the change journey with you, may still be attached to old thinking and methods. You and they may, therefore need help in which direction, backward or forward, to travel.	You are seeing what a new beginning looks and feels like. Embrace the newness of change that has come to be your normal. While you are still adjusting, you are allowing yourself to thrive. Use your wins to help others who are still in Phase 1 and 2 to progress toward Phase 3.

What change are you currently experiencing?

Using the previous pictorial, what phase are you on the Transition Bridge?

There are individuals depending on you to successfully navigate through this change.

- First, write their initials on the Transition Bridge where you believe they are.
- Next, underline 1-2 words, within the table immediately below the Transition Bridge, that describe their feelings.

Looking at the next phase up from where you placed yourself, what is one thing you can do to help yourself transition forward?

___

___

___

Who do you need to help support you through this transition?

___

___

Remember, it is natural that people are at various phases of the Transition Bridge. The positions will differ based on your and other's acceptance of the change. Everyone's journey is unique, therefore there is no right or wrong starting place. The key is recognizing where you are and understanding the differences that exist. Your goal is to navigate within the phases, as you forge toward the Renewal of Phase 3.

Here are a few tips for each of the phases along the "Transition Bridge of Change."

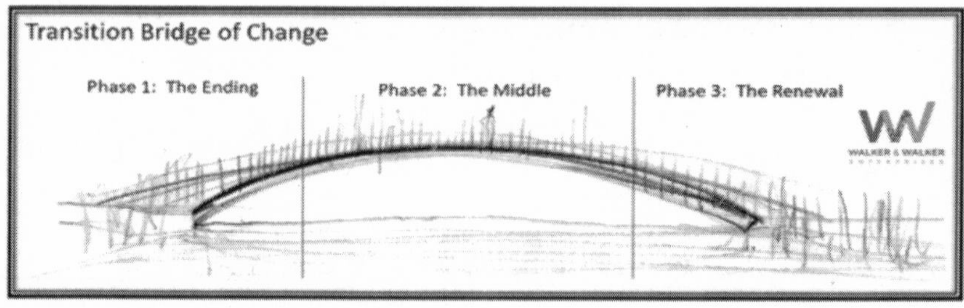

PHASE 1: THE ENDING

- Allow yourself and others time to accept the new and let go of the old way of doing things.
- Listen intently and communicate openly.
- Find the positives, then communicate and re-enforce the wins.
- Clarify and highlight the things that will remain the same.
- Identify those around who are resisting the change. Intently pair them with those who are further along their journey to Phase 3.

PHASE 2: THE MIDDLE

- At times, this phase may seem unproductive, as it may feel that little progress is being made, but don't give up.
- Set a solid direction to provide a sense of calm, reminding yourself and others of your goal.
- Have open discussions on how you and others are feeling.

- Stay motivated and focused by establishing a few short-term goals to see quick wins.
- Help prioritize and deprioritize what may seem overwhelming.
- Capture and celebrate your small wins.

PHASE 3: THE RENEWAL

- Create goals and objectives that will have lasting impacts.
- Do what you say when you say you are going to do it. If you are unable, still communicate the positives. They are there. Find them.
- Create links between personal goals and the goals of the change.
- Establish a way to highlight successes.
- Reward yourself and others for making progress toward embracing the new.
- Communicate, Communicate, Communicate

Stop 3: Be Free Boulevard

BE FREE

Believe in your strengths and open your mind to now explore

Expect moments to have meanings which propel you to soar

Face your fears head on, yet hold them at bay

Release what is not progressing you on today

Experience the unexpected, what you would normally let pass by

Embrace the renewed you who is now free to fly

Welcome to Be Free Boulevard!

THE STOP: THE "BE FREE"

On our journey, this creed serves as a boulevard that pushes you to dig deep within yourself and define what "being free" means to you. The beauty of this stop is that "being free" is defined by you, and only you. Could it be releasing yourself from fear, anxiety, stress, and all other distractions that impede you from living in your purpose and in your happy place? Where and what is your "be free?" Will this boulevard guide you to dream until that dream manifests into reality? By confidently looking forward and relishing in your "be free," you are destined for greatness. The only thing standing in the way of your progression is you, your most unapologetically and most authentically YOU. This stop offers you space to be yourself.

MY STORY: MY "BE FREE"

It was July of 2017 and I opened a box to find a leather binder filled with documents, a business stamp, and a note of congratulations. My personal and organizational coaching and consultancy would journey others through their own transitions of change, and it was now official! My smile spanned from the front door to the back yard. I felt a proud and rewarding sense of release. Through happy tears, I sat on the steps near my kitchen and simply thanked God for this moment, gave gratitude for being in this place, and marveled at the blessing that was staring at me. The name Walker & Walker Enterprises, LLC. was showcased atop each document. I felt myself morph into what felt like an empty canvas ready to receive and give all I had.

Would I allow this new momentum to plant me at the forefront of a movement that empowered the world? Could I pause in this moment to acknowledge my power to soar? Was this what "free" felt like? I sat in this space realizing I had allowed my previous work and fears to handcuff my dreams and aspirations. Could I shift my thinking to now minimize distractions and remain focused? Would this binder confirm there were no boundaries to where I could go and what I could accomplish? How far would I push myself to soar and live each day in my "be free?"

YOUR STORY: YOUR "BE FREE"

What does "being free" mean to you?

____

____

____

____

Describe how you feel when you are free?

____

____

____

____

What is in your way of living with this "free" mindset?

____

____

____

List 3 ways you can shift obstacles and distractions to the sidelines so you remain "free."

Consider, for a second, that being free could be an intentional shift of your thinking.

What if it could offer a:

- deeply rooted feeling of release?
- foundation to build your goals upon?
- shift of distractions from your immediate line of sight?
- sense of awareness for your fears, their triggers, and how best to control them?

Would you then be motivated to find and embrace your "be free?"

Challenge yourself to free your mind, think differently, and welcome "out-of-the box" perspectives. The results may be lasting viewpoints that yield positive and productive results.

Stop 4: Strength Street

STRENGTH

Strength Street is the reminder that you are stronger than you think you are

Tougher than a bag of nails, you'll overcome obstacles near and far

Remembering you are worthy, you are the achiever of your goals

Etched with a legacy of feeding your passion, your heart, and your soul

Next is the ask for strengths from those you've met, both new and old

Grab hold because your strengths will tell a story that's yet to be told

Tack them to the wall and refer back on days you may forget

Hold on to your unique strengths to keep your candle lit

Welcome to Strength Street!

THE STOP: THE STRENGTH

The street of strength embraces the innate characteristics that are ready to help you reach your highest potential. Your strength is that thing people seem to always tell you you're good at. It's that attribute that propels you to excel and that thing you seem to always fall back on. This is Strength Street. This stop is about aligning your path with what makes you shine so that path, your path, remains paved with foundational excellence! This stop is about YOU.

MY STORY: MY STRENGTH

"Something is missing," I thought to myself. In my mind, clients weren't committing fast enough, products were moving slower than expected, and my upcoming women's retreat should have sold out months ago. My savings account was lowering and I wasn't crossing the financial thresholds I projected in my first year of business. I felt I had too large of a network, and that network had too large of a network, to not yet financially thrive. I had proven myself time and time again, however was still falling short of my goals. As I reviewed my social media feeds, it was time to once again live by what I was teaching. It was time to grab hold of the parachute I carried on my leap from corporate. It was bundled with my faith, my experiences, and my strengths. "You are stronger and smarter than what you are being paid for," was a magazine quote I mysteriously and continuously came across each year. Each year's quote found itself mounted atop my last three vision boards. It simply reminded me that my strengths are plentiful. Yes, I am a strategic thinker, a kick-ass certified coach and mentor, an influencer, a powerful speaker, and a loyal friend, to name a few. Though true, how often did I truly list my strengths? How often did I ask this of others? What did I rely on when doubt and fear surfaced? How could I act in my strengths and turn around my own situation?

YOUR STORY: YOUR STRENGTH

What are your top two strengths?

Strength #1___________________________________

Strength #2: __________________________________

How will you use each strength to propel you farther than where you are today?

Strength #1______________________________________

Strength #2: ______________________________________

Identify two friends, co-workers, or even someone you've known for a short period of time. Ask them for two of your strengths, with an example of each. Thank each person for their time and feedback. Document the strengths they each provided below and ask additional persons if your list becomes redundant. Your goal is to have six unique strengths at the conclusion of the exercise, including the two you have already identified.

Remember to pull from these strengths when you find yourself in situations of doubt or indecisiveness. They are what make you stand out, from another person's perspective, thus worth tapping into and fostering. These are examples of greatness that people see in you.

Person #1: ______________________________

Strength #1: ____________________________

Example #1

____

____

Strength #2: ______________________________

Example #2:

____

____

Person #2: ______________________________

Strength #1: ____________________________

Example #1

____

____

Strength #2: ____________________________

Example #2:

____

____

CONGRATULATIONS! You now have six strengths that you will use to power your journey. Believe and trust them. They are uniquely yours.

Stop 5: Truth Tollway

TRUTH

Truth Tollway confronts your inner self before granting your passage through

Reflecting and looking deep within to affirm your intentions are true

Undeterred by those around you and removed from what may not yet be clear

Trying to bridge where you are and where you want to be, despite the rising fear

Harness your inner truth and allow it to guide you to your next tier

Welcome to Truth Tollway!

THE STOP: THE TRUTH

The truth, your truth, and nothing but your truth, so help you God. This certainty opens the tollway to honesty, which is oftentimes difficult to give and to receive. This stop is about allowing inner truth to guide your next steps. It's about being "real" with yourself in efforts to truly reach your goal of happiness. It's about moving distractions to the sidelines and selfishly looking inside as your top priority. It's about being true to you and living authentically in what brings you a fulfillment of peace.

MY STORY: MY TRUTH

I have created next year's budget and there are some changes we will see in the next few months. Those were the sentiments of my direct manager, as he outlined the shift of being acquired by a smaller company and the link to my position as a senior employee on the leadership team. As I jumped in to help him summarize the words he so delicately attempted to declare, the organization was being downsized and my role was being eliminated in six months' time, if I did not choose to take an opportunity in another city. My current responsibilities would be taken on by a peer, and I was to create a seamless transition plan for my replacement and my staff. The feelings were not that of disbelief, because I had known we were soon reducing costs, with headcount as part of the plan. The emotions were that of anxiousness, given the reality of yes, this is happening. Another feeling was fear, and then of "what now?" What was my inner truth? I had known this was coming and had given thought to whether my principles and values would fit into the new organization. I had balanced my considerations of potentially moving to a new state with a 5-year old and had outlined what compromises would need to be made. It was time for me to pause and find my truth. Would this nourish me mentally, emotionally, and progressively within my career? What was my truth? What could I live with, as I also quested to live free?

YOUR STORY: YOUR TRUTH

What are two core principles or values that govern you?

____

____

____

Why are they so important?

____

____

____

What is one decision you are currently contemplating?

____

____

____

What about this decision is keeping you awake at night?

____

____

____

Which of your core values or principles will this decision stand upon?

____

____

____

What does a successful decision, in this situation, look and feel like to you?

____

____

____

Who can you leverage for support in helping you reach your best decision?

____

____

____

What specifically will you ask this person to do, by way of supporting you?

____

____

____

If you were honest with yourself and had to make your decision today on what you were contemplating in this situation, what would it be?

___

___

___

Who will your decision impact and how?

___

___

___

Does this decision allow you to live in the truth of the two core principles or values that you wrote above, which govern you?

___

___

___

Stop 6: Forgiveness Freeway

FORGIVENESS

Forgiveness Freeway sometimes journeys you to lands which are unknown

Opening your eyes to self-mercy, with a focus on what you've previously been shown

Remembering you have control over yourself, which is where forgiveness must start

Giving freely of you mind, your spirit, and your heart

It's time to acknowledge where you are and find lessons in what didn't work so well

Venture upon a new journey to make memories you'll one day tell

Empower others to join you by inviting them to" Forgiveness Freeway" as well

Now it's time to let go of what you may or may not have done

Exercise the strength to acknowledge that your new journey has only just begun

Soon your inner peace will absolve you of any guilt you may still feel

Start with you by commencing a process that allows you to simply heal

Welcome to Forgiveness Freeway!

THE STOP: THE FORGIVENESS

Sometimes forgiveness feels like the most impossible freeway to navigate, though the power of forgiveness is unmatched. It is selfless and is solely for you. Forgiveness offers healing effects and is the notion to not forget, but to remember without malice or judgement. This stop is the promise that your place of peace will resonate through your mind, body, and soul, for not only yourself, but for others you are also able to forgive.

MY STORY: MY FORGIVENESS

"God has already forgiven you Lolita. Now is the time for you to forgive yourself," a voice said softly, yet firmly into my ear. A graduate school classmate had reconnected by phone, in this very moment, after 14 years from when we'd last spoken. She reminded me of this message just moments before I walked into the court house for my divorce proceedings. With my mom at my side in the passenger seat, I had no clue how emotional this day would actually be. This is not how I'd imagined the proceedings. Through tears, I answered the judge's questions and next, watched as my mom mounted the witness stand. In that moment, I somehow blocked the courtroom of strangers awaiting their turn to end their union. Eyes locked on the judge, I could not look left, toward where my husband sat silently. I had not yet forgiven him for the gaps of what I thought necessary of a husband. I could not face myself. I had not yet forgiven me for the part I owned for the dissolution. I was holding on to so much and, in that moment, all I could think was whether I had removed every distraction to be one half of the pair we vowed to be forever.

Is this what I had prayed for? Had my lack of forgiveness barricaded my progression forward? Were the feelings I had a build-up of frustration, communication-gone-wrong, and emptiness? Could we each forgive and just completely move on? Could I receive my classmate's words? Ten minutes and a few questions later, the judge hit her gavel and after ten years of friendship and five years of marriage, she sent us away, divorced. Seated in the hallway, I took a deep breath in of the gratitude I had for a strong support system and for the strength God had granted me to still help others as I journeyed through my own storm.

Next was a deep breath out to release the fear, anxiety, and resentment I was still holding. Just like that, it was done and it was time to simply forgive, yet there was nothing simple about it. Was this the pitstop where forgiveness offered me a freeway to release the guilt leading up to these events? Was there a way to remove resentment and begin looking ahead as a co-parenting pair? How could I be completely present to travel my Forgiveness Freeway?

YOUR STORY: YOUR FORGIVENESS

What is one thing that you are holding onto?

____

____

____

____

Who do you blame for what you are holding on to?

What role did you play? *Remember this question is about you. I am asking you to think about your accountability and ownership within the situation.*

What is in your control that will help you move on?

What will you intentionally do to forgive yourself, or the someone you blamed above, to move on today?

Checking In

Hello There! The Change Train is six stops in on our journey, marking the halfway point in the book. **It's check-in time.**

Thus far, you've journeyed through transition, be free, strength, truth, and forgiveness. Are the stops along your journey intertwining to bring you self-awareness and discovery?

We are now on our way to the "act" and "thrive" regions of the book. If you need a break, please take one, as it is totally understandable. This book uses a good portion of brain power, challenges your mind, takes you to uncomfortable stops, and forces you to lands of unknown.

Give yourself moments to breathe and recollect, if needed. Sit on it for an hour, a day, or even a week. Reread what you have written thus far and take it in. Here, and in the rear of the book, are additional whitespaces to write discoveries, notes, & recollections you've had along the way.

ACT.

Welcome to the terrain of Act.

Act is defined as to move and behave in a certain way.

The next five stops will help you INTENTIONALLY act with clarity, purpose, and accountability.

Stop 7: Focus Fairway

FOCUS

Focus Fairway journeys through fear and will handcuff progression if you allow

Onboard your mind to an emphasis on what is required of you right now

Create your vision for what lies ahead, assign a clear and manageable plan

Un-think self-limiting beliefs because the shift is right in your hands

Share where you are going and I'll see you atop the winners stand

Welcome to Focus Fairway!

THE STOP: THE FOCUS

In the midst of circumstance, it is oftentimes difficult to see and think clearly. Though we want to operate in the clarity of right now, aspects such as egos or past experiences can cloud where we know we want to be. This stop is your "Focus Fairway" and provides access to a highway of clarity and direction in the midst of everything around you. This stop challenges you to move attention toward your goals. At Stop 9, we will talk of clarity in a bit more detail, however at this stop, let's think about a time where you had a group of dominos crowding your space. Each domino was vying for your attention and your only goal was to avoid knocking one down, which would send the remainder to a collapse and an unstoppable path of destruction.

MY STORY: MY FOCUS

"I know I am not coming back home," were the words my dad spoke as my almost two-year-old and I visited him in the hospital immediately after landing in Baltimore. He had gone in for a routine doctor visit and had been immediately admitted after reacting negatively to contrast dye pre-MRI. At a military hospital, I gazed into his grey eyes and could tell he was not the same man I'd known for 36 years. My forever-guy was different. A silent panic shot throughout my body, however that amazingly genuine smile and that tight hold onto his grandson, reminded me he was still there. He was my daddy, despite what I could physically see were effects of the many drugs the doctors had prescribed. This was the first moment I physically and mentally accepted my dad had cancer, after being diagnosed at stage 4 prostate cancer 6 years prior. With an original 8-month expectancy to live, to see him years prior to this day, was to not recognize there was cancer amid his bones and within his body. He was merely my dad and nothing seemed different until today. His hospital visit lasted a few weeks, rehabilitation followed, and during that stay, God decided his last stop would be to find comfort at home with his family. His memory was fading, he was transitioning into a new spirit, and my mom was the amazing support that only a strong wife could be. I was a little over an hour away with a new job, a new husband, a new child, in what felt like a strange new land. It was nothing but God that allowed these moments of clarity, of trials, of tribulations, of growth, of love, of change. I look back and ask myself, "how did I focus in the midst of that emotional chaos?" What was my priority and how did I craft a plan to achieve what was most important? What help did I need? Who was I supporting and what did they need of me? How did I stack the dominos to prevent them from falling at the same time?

YOUR STORY: YOUR FOCUS

In the blank space on each domino, write four situations that are currently competing for your focus, and in your mind, are each equally important.

For each domino, what is specifically needed **from you**?

Domino #1:

Domino #2:

Domino #3:

Domino #4:

What is the worst thing that would happen if you didn't focus as much time on:

Domino #1?

Domino #2?

Domino #3?

Domino #4?

Now ask yourself, how likely is it that the "worst thing" is really going to happen and why?

Domino #1?

Domino #2?

Domino #3?

Domino #4?

Lastly, reprioritize your dominos, focusing on what is specifically needed **from you** in each situation. In the middle of each, write the name of a person who can help support you, specifically with what you wrote above.

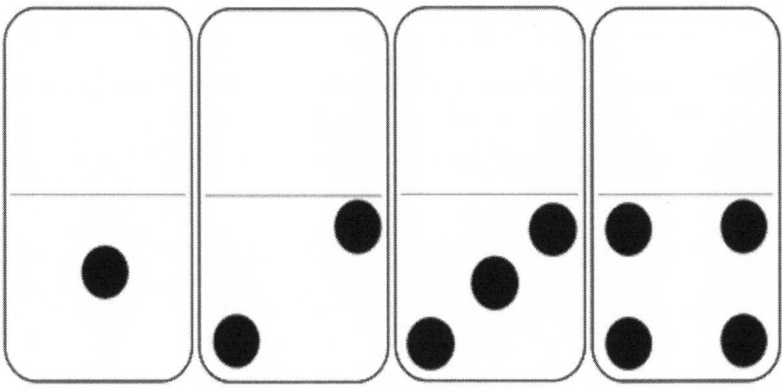

Did your focus areas shift? ___________________________

It's highly likely that they did. This is a good thing. If nothing more, you have added a bit of clarity, which is always a winner. When you get granular with the exact role you play within each domino, you are able to release things that are not immediate priorities. You are also able to allow others to take on tasks they are willing to help with.

Occasionally, we find ourselves holding onto dominos simply because we want to maintain control. It is definitely difficult to let go of control. I can attest! Consider this. Think of how you feel when others try to control you and handcuff your capabilities. You may discover that when you let go of even an inch of control for doing things your exact way, you find a newfound support who is willing to help you lessen the pressures weighing you down. Ultimately, you may realize that your support will reinforce your dominos to remain upright. Challenge yourself to stay clear and directionally focused on what is truly important for you to take on. To focus is to let go of fear and control. Give yourself permission to focus and uncuff both yourself and your progression.

Stop 8: Unexpected Underpass

UNEXPECTED

Unexpected is oftentimes an underpass where you simply want to run and hide

No planning or considerations, this stop often takes you by surprise

Etched as a new adventure and a momentary pause that came your way

Xerox copies of past experiences may give direction whether you go or if you stay

Pushed to the edge to determine what consequences are lurking nearby

Experiencing moments which may afford you something new to try

Carry with you the faith and values you vowed to constantly uphold

Take a pause and a breath, then take all within your control

Embrace the newness you've found on Unexpected Underpass

Direct your next steps to create memories that will last

Welcome to Unexpected Underpass!

THE STOP: THE UNEXPECTED

At this stop, you'll consider how you handle the unexpected, while not losing focus of what is important. No planning and no control, the unexpected takes you out of your comfort zone. This "unexpected underpass" offers an opportunity to live in that moment, as scary or exciting as it may be. Will you retreat or figure out a plan b to get to your end destination? How will you make your best happen in the midst of the unexpected?

MY STORY: MY UNEXPECTED

The music was blasting in the background, ladies were lined on both sides, and I danced down the middle in my bright green maternity dress with sparkly 4-inch heels. The soul train line was full of laughter as we celebrated the 47th regional conference of my sorority, where planning was a year in the making. With the planning team celebrating success, giving birth to my son was the last thing on my mind. I was at week 31 and the plan was to enjoy a few relaxing vacation days at home before jumping into my normal hustle and bustle. I had taken off work, had sleep on my brain, and I was ready for it all. I had not yet realized that the very next day, April 23, 2012, my son would be born at 1lb15oz.

During a routine doctor visit that I nearly cancelled, preeclampsia was discovered. Walker was ready to create his space in this world. "Be prepared to have your son in 72 hours," the nurse said with a smile. Next, she noted 24 hours and not too long after, she calmly said, "Your baby is stressed, so we are going to take him now." "OK," was our response, "let's get him out of there." No car seat, no hospital bag, no anxiously awaiting family members, my husband and I were gearing up to be first-time parents in a matter of minutes. How exciting, how scary, how unexpected, how real. What would this new world look like? Would the fun times be instantly over? Would this situation stress me to a point where everyone around was a target for my frustration and fear?

YOUR STORY: YOUR UNEXPECTED

We are unable to predict the unexpected, however when the unexpected does occur, we can trigger ourselves to pause, take a step back, and allow time to settle, just a bit. Let's think back to a time where you were on an Unexpected Underpass. What was happening?

____

____

____

How did you feel?

____

____

____

What was your reaction?

____

____

____

Now that the unexpected has passed and you are thinking back, could you have had a different response that may have caused less stress and anxiety to you and others? __________________________________

What was happening in the moment when you could have triggered that new response?

____

____

____

____

When you are feeling emotions of ___________________ or ________________________________, what can you do in those moments to create a calming refocus to what is important?

____

____

____

____

____

____

____

____

Stop 9: Clarity Cul-de-Sac

CLARITY

Clarity Cul-de-sac can quickly shift to a dead end with no outlet if you allow

Lacking focus, positivity, and certainty in your here and now

Ask yourself tough questions and penetrate where you need to go

Relax your emotions and allow your intuition to simply flow

Insist on tackling what's important to push you forward toward your goal

Transparent with your support to avoid falling down a dark hole

Yield to block anything that attempts to take what's in your control

Welcome to Clarity Cul-de-Sac!

THE STOP: THE CLARITY

Here, you've arrived at the stop where getting clear is not always picture perfect. Oftentimes you may find yourself in the midst of your circumstances and unable to see through the fog of distractions, opinions of others, egos, and other hurdles that surface at the most inopportune times. The path is clear, yet your perception is unclear and full of fog. This is where the clarity of who, what, when, where, why, and how become extremely helpful.

MY STORY: MY CLARITY

I arrived home to his clothes no longer in the closet or the sounds of snores during the night. Reality quickly set in that our separation would soon change to divorce. The months of missed communication and unfounded assumptions moved us into a space we never imagined after only five short years of marriage. What happened to the ten years of prior fun, excitement, and love? The initial physical move of only a few miles away, shifted to his permanent move, a few interstates away. The ending felt rushed and was as clear as overcast clouds above mountains. Through the fog, we moved outside of ourselves to maintain an amicable friendship, which allowed the most seamless transition for our son. In the midst of this new circumstance, how would I clear the chaos in my mind? How could I declutter the opinions of others, on both sides, to truly sort what was important to me, my family, and where I wanted and needed to be?

YOUR STORY: YOUR CLARITY

I want to help maximize your time in Clarity Cul-de-sac. Let's push distractions aside and bring clarity to what is important to you and your future. Think about a goal. Try to be specific and granular in your focus. **Why?** Because when you are clear and understand the context, you can draw a connection to your desired outcomes. So, let's give it a try by composing, what I call a "clarity statement."

Let's drill down to grab a few key components.

- **Who** is responsible for where you want to be? The answer is you, so consider this a freebie!
- **What** are you solving for as you move toward embracing this new change?
- **When** will this change take place?
- **Where** will you do the work to prepare for the change?
- **Why** is transitioning through this space so critical for the outcome of where you want to be?
- **How** will you achieve your goal?

EXAMPLE 1:

My Change: My divorce is final and the new change of sharing my son for the holidays is a bit overwhelming to me.

My Clarity Statement: By February 2017, with a calendar and knowledge of past experiences, I will have drafted an electronic co-parenting plan, by separating the holidays to maintain the traditions most important to each of us.

EXAMPLE 2:

My Change: The brand I've worked on for years is being divested to a smaller, less recognized company, with a different culture.

My Clarity Statement: By January 2017, during my working hours, I will ensure my employees are positively shifting toward the new culture, by engaging them in the creation of standards that drive clarity during the integration.

EXAMPLE 3:

My Change: I leaped to start my new coaching and consulting business and am unsure of what to do next.

My Clarity Statement: By January 2018, within a 15-mile radius, I will have facilitated 2 workshops, using my proprietary methodologies to help people remove distractions and make the best decisions for change scenarios.

Let's practice using your example:

What is Your Change?

____

____

____

____

What is Your Clarity Statement?

____

____

____

____

In your example, remember to check for the presence of Who, What, When, Where, Why, and How.

- **Who** is responsible for where you want to be?
- **What** are you solving for as you move toward embracing this new change?
- **When** will this change take place?
- **Where** will you do the work to prepare for the change?
- **Why** is transitioning through this space so critical for the outcome of where you want to be?
- **How** will you achieve your goal?

Congratulations! You now have a strong clarity statement to serve as the covering necessary to lead your work!

When we are unclear, we find ourselves in a bottomless and frustrating pit of uncertainty and redundancy. Oftentimes we believe we have a plan, yet continue to spin. The plan is either not specific enough or not yet linked to our desired outcomes. When we can reference a clear and attainable goal, we shift toward actions and support. This is where the work truly happens.

Stop 10: Breathe Boulevard

BREATHE

Breathe in deeply and journey to a boulevard of clean thoughts with a momentary pause

Reflect in the moment to gift yourself an advanced applause…. For

Exhaling negative energy which could hinder your movement ahead

Adjusting your thoughts to positivity, so in your mind you can embed

The calm, the peace, and the clarity you need to maneuver within this space

Hover over your breakthrough, you are re-centered and acting at a slower pace

Embrace the unapologetic decisions you will now face

Welcome to Breathe Boulevard!

THE STOP: THE BREATH

Breathing offers our cells a new supply of oxygen so they can constantly and consistently produce energy. We occasionally find ourselves needing to trigger a momentary pause, where an intentional deep breath becomes the boulevard to recollect our thoughts and channel our energy for clear and concise decision-making.

MY STORY: MY BREATH

It was year eight at my first job out of college and I was seated in an Associate Director's (AD) office outlining three things I needed to stay employed with this Fortune 500 company. How did I get here? "Wow, I am valued," is what I slowly understood, as the butterflies fluttered out of control in my belly. There was yet a confidence in my spirit, a pen and pad in front of me, and wonder in my mind, as I sat at the wood circular table in his office. It was less than 24 hours after I said an early good-bye to a female senior HR leader. Immediately after facilitating an offsite meeting with my staff, I was asked to meet the AD in his office. I watched as he pulled back a sliding dry erase board to reveal the numbers and explanations he had pre-worked for this moment. I was 31 years old.

There was a resenting part of me that drifted as he spoke, wondering why it had taken so long to have this particular discussion with my well-respected senior mentor within the organization. He wanted to discuss what I needed to stay with this company. Was it the "too good to be true" job offer I had in front of me or the mystery sponsor(s) I didn't know were talking on my behalf? Was it the word from this amazing woman leader who made a phone call to get this discussion in motion? or was it quite simply, the amazing talents, work ethic, and continued results that made me a great fit with the company? I felt scared, had feelings of confusion, yet I felt valued, important, and worthy. My heart was racing, yet I still wanted to present a calm. How do I slow things down and find a way to breathe with this new information? There were thoughts surrounding me, but how could I exhale when there was no private room for my "call-a-parent-moment?" How would I sift through the numbers and scenarios that were competing for space in my brain?

YOUR STORY: YOUR BREATH

What situation have you had or are currently having, where you may feel boxed in for a decision?

____

____

____

What is making you feel boxed in?

____

____

____

What does/did your body feel in that moment?

____

____

____

What happens if you intentionally choose to pause, allow silence, slow down, and breathe, right there in that moment?

____

____

____

What happens if you say you need time to think and will get back with an answer?

____

____

____

Remember, breathing gives you the oxygen you need to make clear decisions. You own your space and your response. Give yourself permission to take those moments. Pause, breathe, and collect yourself before you rush into anything. Remind yourself that there is power in uncomfortable silence, as my daddy would oftentimes remind me.

Stop 11: Leaping Lane

LEAPING

Latch on to your faith and strengths, then soar to even greater heights

Expect ups and downs on this journey that will bring your dreams to life

Assess your progress along the way, then adjust to meet your goals

Prepare to live in your greatness, for it will soon begin to unfold

Ignite your inner strength, because to leap is uncertainty at its height

Navigate the rocky path of nervousness and doubt that will quickly line your sight

Grab hold of your past and present experiences to be your guiding light

Welcome to Leaping Lane!

THE STOP: THE LEAP

Uncertainty, fear, excitement, and unrealized dreams, all border this stop. Leaping Lane packs an armor for your success as you close your eyes, scoot out of your own way, and leap into the lane of unknown. This is where you pull from a collective of your faith, strengths, and support, to act as a parachute that will guide your journey to soar. You will slow to a descent that places you right where you need to be. This stop is about mustering up the courage to follow your instincts, despite the rocky path you may travel to reach the pinnacle of discomfort. This is from where you will leap.

MY STORY: MY LEAP

"Thank you, Ms. Walker. I enjoyed our conversation today. When you are ready to re-engage, please dial me directly." These were the words of the fourth recruiter this week and the sentiments of the prior three, who were connecting me to full-time corporate positions that would start immediately. While excited at each opportunity presented, I informed each caller that I had a full-time job as an entrepreneur and how they could best benefit from the services of Walker & Walker Enterprises, my company of change, coaching, and consultancy. As I took a few deep breaths after each call, I had so many mixed emotions. Pulses of excitement, moments of fear, butterflies of uncertainty, and doses of reality all played ping pong in my head. With each play of back and forth, I was pushed to leap further into my passion, my full-time commitment, and my career. In my mind, I simply needed the visibility and awareness to burst my explosive and dynamic movement toward the right person, in the right place. Were my products and services dynamic enough to surface to the top of this crowded coaching and speaking space? Would my savings take me far enough to maintain my standard of living, while following my dream? Did I have enough connections to soar beyond the place I stood? Was leaping worth the sacrifice? Was I making the right decision for my son and I?

YOUR STORY – YOUR LEAP

If there were no boundaries, what dream would you be living?

Who would you have beside you?

What is blocking you from living that dream today?

What are two ways you can work to move those blocks out of your way?

What is one thing you will do within this week to chip away at the block before you?

___

___

___

What are you losing by not living your dream today?

___

___

___

Are you willing to continue experiencing that loss?

___

What's the worst thing that can happen if you leap into your dream today?

___

___

___

How likely is it that this worst thing will happen if you create a clear plan to mitigate it?

___

___

___

Leap! It is worth the results. Remember, you are not in it alone.

THRIVE.

Welcome to the terrain of Thrive.

Thrive is defined as to flourish and prosper.

The final six stops await you. They will help you leap to your unknown. They will help you soar.

Stop 12: Acceptance Avenue

ACCEPTANCE

Acceptance is the avenue that plays tricks on what you know is true

Challenging your self-assurance, occasionally questioning what makes you, you

Coming to a place you'll take inventory of your beliefs and of your faith

Expand your list of strengths to use as wallpaper in your sacred space

Parade the renewed you who sees positives in the bad and in the good

Train your mind to acknowledge what will soon be understood

Allow yourself to be embraced not by doubt, nor by fear

Nourish your soul to rebuild your foundation and set the rules to which you'll adhere

Change your narrative to be receptive of gifts that are yours and are unique

Exude the will to follow your inner voice and accept all that you seek

Welcome to Acceptance Avenue!

THE STOP: THE ACCEPTANCE

Acceptance Avenue is a not a path of giving up, but instead, one of being aware of what is and then leveraging that to arrive at what will be. This avenue is where affirmations turn into receiving the gifts God has afforded you. My challenge to you is to grab acceptance and use it as a footstool to soar. This stop checks what acceptance means to you, while offering a few considerations to maneuver in this space. Consider acceptance as receiving your blessings so you may thrive in your current situation. Consider it an initial step in your quest to shift toward a higher plane.

At this stop, you will acknowledge that your strengths separate you from the crowd and that any person's acceptance of you doesn't redirect the ownership you have to trust and accept what is. When you accept the challenges and triumphs in your life as lessons along your journey, you shift your thinking from the obstacles that lay ahead, to the affirmative of what can and will be. Acceptance offers you happiness and moves you out of your own way, in spite of what anyone else does or says. You are special, you are unique, and you are made in an image of perfection. Open your mind to accept this reality and you will travel this avenue with ease.

MY STORY: MY ACCEPTANCE

It was mid-day and there was a message notification that buzzed my phone. I looked closer to see it was sent from a good friend, author, and fellow Morgan State Alumni, a few hours after his wife and I conversed of a recent situation that had become a constant distraction in my mind. I had begun to challenge my thoughts on work, those I interact with, and how I would move forward with my business.

His text message profoundly read, "Believe in yourself, bet on yourself. You have all the answers you need right there inside of you. Do not be guided or driven by doubt or fear, but reach into your core and be what you dreamed of before you leaped off the ledge. This is no time to question whether or not you were put here to change the world, and this is certainly no time to be shackled by unfruitful, unprolific, imbalanced energy. When we ignore our intuition, we falter and fail every time because that intuition is God speaking his truth to you. I pray you come to see how bright your light really is, and that you do not make the mistake of dimming it for fear that you are not who that voice says you are. Accept it. Believe the voice and do not step down from your rightful place in this world."

Could I accept that this was the path God intended me to walk? Could I move out of my own way to accept me, in this time, this space, and with these words? What would I do with this newfound acceptance?

YOUR STORY: YOUR ACCEPTANCE

Head back to Stop 4: Strength Street, to re-write your six strengths below.

______________________________, ___________________________,

______________________________, ___________________________,

______________________________ & ________________________.

Choose two of the strengths that have helped you overcome an obstacle?

Strength #1:

____

Strength #2:

____

How have these strengths assisted you in helping someone else?

Strength #1:

____

____

Strength #2:

____

____

How will these strengths help you in a situation you are currently dealing with?

Strength #1:

____

____

Strength #2:

____

____

Please fill in the blanks, using the guidance within the parentheses.

I am ____
(your name)

and I accept that I am _________________________
(strength #1),

I am ____
(strength #2),

I am ____
(strength #3),

I am ____
(strength #4).

I am ____
(strength 5)

& I am ______________________________________
(strength 6).

I know these are gifts bestowed upon me and will help me accept who I am and where I want to be.

In my current situation of

____

____

____

(a brief summary of one situation you are currently experiencing), I am grateful for two strengths in particular,

____

(choose any strength) and ________________________

(choose any strength).

I will use them to

____

____

____

____

(insert goal related to your situation).

I accept where I am, know where I have been, and will use my strengths to help me meet the goals of where I want to be, despite who I may leave on the sidelines throughout my journey. I accept these things of myself so I do not resort to needing acceptance from others. I, therefore, accept my intention to soar.

When you have completed your strength and affirmation work in this section, please read your completed statements aloud. Own it and believe it. This is YOUR affirmation of strengths.

Stop 13: Accountability Access Road

ACCOUNTABILITY

At the start of Accountability Access Road is a clear purpose that will guide your way

Confident you'll identify someone you trust and want to stay

Consider that this person must tell you what you need, not want to hear

Open to challenge one another's hesitations and occasional fears

Undeterred by blocks and limiting beliefs, this person is a partner who elevates your mind

No intention of allowing complacency, this person is deliberate in helping you shine

Tracking your commitments and challenging your gaps beginning right here and now

Addressing questions of who, what, when, where, why, and how

Back to the foundation of you, this is what to expect and what to give

Igniting your purpose, clarity, and actions of how you want to live

Learning accountability is a process of action and support to help you and others win

Invert the image you see in the mirror and this is where you must begin

Think of a clear plan and choose support who will bring your vision to fruition

You will begin to hold yourself to a higher standard - one which is driven by intention

Welcome to Accountability Access Road!

THE STOP: THE ACCOUNTABILITY

Accountability Access Road can intersect with Focus Fairway and Partnership Parkway when you least expect. It's where the rubber meets the road and where you leap from talking about it to being about it! The access to accountability begins with you being clear on expectations and at the onset, being liable for self. It's where you commit to yourself and others what you will do, the support you need specifically from them, and by when you are committed to be held answerable to your goals. Scary right? Of course!

When you shift to become accountable for others, this access road provides a pathway to steer them toward their goals, no matter what distractions may surface. The road offers a partnership that holds each person's feet to the fire for the responsibilities they have agreed upon.

This road is a necessary stop on your journey to truly being free. At first glance, the light may appear dim as you peek down Accountability Access Road, however there is a bright excitement that opens up as you journey farther. **Keep going, you are almost there!**

MY STORY: MY ACCOUNTABILITY

My phone buzzed at 9:13pm and I was in bed praying for a clear mind to lead me on a path of clarity as I strategized how to increase my company's brand awareness. After a while and when I was ready to receive, I grabbed the phone to see an unfamiliar number attached to a simple text message that stated, "Hi, I know it's late, I got your number from a friend. Do you have time tomorrow after 4 to do a radio interview about Walker & Walker Enterprises? It will air in a few days and I am excited to speak with you about your business and upcoming events…."

Wait, what? I think it's real but let me read it again. The smile that spread beyond dimple to dimple was affixed for at least 15 minutes as I called my mom and also left a message for the gentleman who connected this woman to me. I would be held accountable to those who helped me get to this place, to listeners who were new to my work, and to myself, as I communicate clearly on what brought me so much passion and fulfillment. How can I make this dynamic woman part of my accountability circle? I decided that I would affirm on air, that I WILL BE a published author by Christmas 2018. Was I ready to take responsibility for this leap with only 8 months to my accountability date? Was this random feeling one of fear or even a perceived threat of not meeting my goal?

YOUR STORY: YOUR ACCOUNTABILITY

The below paragraph grants an access road of accountable for your plans throughout the weeks. I developed this template for my two-week plans because it drives the clarity I need for accountability, ownership, and commitment to myself and my accountability partner.

My accountability partner is

____

(insert name), who will hold me accountable to

____

____

____

(insert what you are committing to do) by

____

(insert date). We will meet

____

(insert frequency), on

____

(insert day), where

____

(accountability partners' name) will

____

____

____

____

(insert specifically what this person will do to hold you accountable) to hold me accountable to my goal.

EXAMPLE:

My accountability partner is **MW,** who will hold me accountable to **drive excitement of my book launch, its content, and pre-sales for the holiday** by **December 1, 2018**. We will meet **the 2nd Sunday of each month at the Uptown Diner,** where **MW** will **review my timeline and give coaching for media management** to follow.

The key to maintaining accountability is to intersect it with Communication Circle. Be sure to follow up with your identified accountability partner so they are clear on what you are seeking from them. This also allows you to confirm they are able and willing to take on that responsibility.

Stop 14: Partnership Parkway

PARTNERSHIP

Peruse Partnership Parkway to catch a glimpse of far and near

Ask yourself who you'd invite on your journey if you didn't have any fear

Remind yourself there are no rules and that no one is exempt

Try your best to make constructive conversations with everyone who attempts

Never fall short on saying "thank you" or "I appreciate you very much"

Earn the respect of others you know, you love, and you trust

Relish in knowing that no one progresses by doing it all alone

Stand firm, push forward, and leave no unturned stone

Here ready and waiting is a partner that yearns to see you succeed

Inspired by your determination, courage, and trust in the "Be Free" Creed

Partner with those who will push you to continuously lead

Welcome to Partnership Parkway!

THE STOP: THE PARTNERSHIP

When some think of partnership, they think of giving up a piece of their control. This stop encourages you to view partnerships as parkways to relationships, connections, and joint goals to your endeavors. This stop helps you practice the art of saying thank you and then accepting when someone wants to help you achieve success.

MY STORY: MY PARTNERSHIP

I glanced over to notice money deposited into my bank account! Nice, but hmmmm, the deposit had not been made by me. I looked closer to see who sent this unexpected gift. Though we'd known each other for years, had coached and mentored one other during several personal and professional situations, I was a bit surprised. It was only a few moments earlier that we'd hung up from a conversation about my business, its progression, and plans to move it forward, yet he had not mentioned sending any money. I sent a text to that good friend and asked if he was making a deposit for his wife to attend my upcoming Women's Weekend Renewal & Training Retreat. His response was breathtaking. "Just some drops into your dream. I should be doing more but figured I would start here." He mentioned that when he was able to partner in other ways, he would make it happen. As I thanked him with tears rolling down my face, he texted, "you are very welcome and please don't over think or over thank." Could I pause, say thank you, and simply marvel in my moment of this amazing partnership, where our joint goal was success for my company? Was this first monetary investment into Walker & Walker Enterprises, LLC. another confirmation that I was on the right path with my mission and vision? Did my passion, energy, and what he knew of my work ethic solidify a partnership before we had even spoken? Were there any expectations within our new partnership toward success?

YOUR STORY: YOUR PARTNERSHIP

If you are seeking a partner to journey with you for a specific endeavor, here's food for thought.

For what reason are you seeking a partner?

____

____

____

Write down a list of four persons who you would trust to meet the needs you have written above

Person #1

____

Person #2

____

Person #3

____

Person #4

____

Write a goal you would have for each person, to whom you may want to partner

Person #1

Person #2

Person #3

Person #4

What role would you play in the partnership?

What would they need to provide, if anything, to enter into a partnership with you?

What's in it for them?

Now that you are clear, consider reaching out using the talking points you have outlined above.

Here's another consideration. Have you been blessed with a partner you did not specifically seek, but has shown support in your quest to meet one of your goals?

____

What was your reaction?

____

____

____

Have you said Thank You for their partnership and support?

____

Take this opportunity to re-engage with that person and thank them again for being a partner when you least expected it. Tell them what their partnership did toward you achieving your goals.

____

____

____

What is the date and time you have confirmed you will meet?

____

____

____

Lock it in your calendar and be grateful for this "Partnership Parkway."

Stop 15: Communication Circle

COMMUNICATION

Communication is the circle that doubles as a two-way lane

Occupied by many truths, which may or may not cause you pain

Maneuvering in this open space of honesty for those who you are with

Maintaining a dialogue of transparency will hone in on this special gift

Uncut and unfiltered, occasional fear and doubt may dance in your head

Notwithstanding emotions of the words and gestures that were or were not said

It could be your ego or even your limiting beliefs that block your way

Communication is at the heart of understanding if you should or should not stay

Accept your "right now" to be in this moment, and check your values are still aligned

Tackle a clear goal you want to achieve so everyone involved is able to shine

Instruct yourself to listen even more than you will speak

Onboard patience, unleash confidence, and be willing to compromise, for it doesn't make you weak

Nourishing your relationships with healthy communication is something we will all, at some point seek

Welcome to Communication Circle!

THE STOP: THE COMMUNICATION

This stop surfaces an ever-so-slippery-slope. No matter the relationship, whether friend, business partner, marriage, or other, the act of articulating what's on your mind to another person, will almost always result in a communication gap of some sort, if not careful. Transmitting your brain's thoughts in such a way where the essence of what you are trying to say is received, is the simplest way to summarize this stop. There is, yet nothing simply about it. Whether verbal, written, gestures, or technology, communication is in fact, a circle with a beginning and no end. It is a continuous and intentional interaction between two or more persons. It exchanges ideas, where all parties must make the conscious choice to give and to receive. Communication gets a bit tricky, however, as does anything. What you put work into will improve over time, IF you really want it to.

MY STORY: MY COMMUNICATION

"I feel like a single father," he said, as he described his emotion. We had recently relocated to a new state, I was in a new role, in a new business unit, with new people, a new baby, a sorority sister who was battling cancer and a dad, who lived over an hour away, coping with the same disease at stage 4. I was once again, a small fish, in a big pond, after 13 years of building credibility, trust, and results. Late nights in the office, traveling back and forth to homes and hospitals, and passing out as soon as I got home, became commonplace events during this time.

What I didn't immediately appreciate was the enormous change my husband was also experiencing: the relocation from a city where he was born, raised, and lived his entire life, limited personal connections in our new city, a job that was not his first choice, and our first child that he wanted to feel the comfort of being around family at all times. What I also didn't readily appreciate was how much of my time, energy, and commitment the world around me needed. I undervalued how much of me I truly needed. I also had not recognized how much I was looking for others to give to me. Work, home, and life…everything seemed so important and my dominos were beginning to fall. How would we communicate in the midst of our busy lives? How would we express the unsaid words and expectations we had for one another that were still unmet? How should we communicate beyond what was outwardly said? How do we not fall on the slippery slope of communication circle?

YOUR STORY: YOUR COMMUNICATION

(a) What is one thing that you've been holding on to that may be helpful for you to communicate about or with someone?

____

____

____

(b) Who is the someone you will communicate with?

____

(c) When is a good, quiet time, where all parties can chat face to face or via a live web meeting?

____

____

(d) When you get together, what are three topics you would like to chat within the conversation?

Topic #1:

____

Topic #2:

____

Topic #3:

____

(e) What do you hope will result from the conversation?

____

____

____

____

(f) Is this an emotional topic for either of you and why?

____

____

____

____

(g)What will you do in the conversation, if you feel yourself becoming overly emotional and veering off topic?

(h) What will you do in the conversation, if the other party becomes overly emotional and veers off topic?

Now that you have thought about this a bit, consider calling the person you outlined in letter (b) above with this script, or a variation that best fits your situation. The key at this stop is to open the lines of communication and keep the circle moving continuously as your relationship grows.

Hi

(b), I have been thinking a lot about

(a) and would love to talk to you about it. I recognize this may be an emotional topic for both of us (if true), however my goal is to do a lot of listening, be open, honest, and hopefully

(e). Would that conversation be something you would be open to?

In our conversation, I would love to talk about

(d) and was wondering if there was anything that you too wanted to connect on.

I was hoping you were available

(c) for us to talk face-to-face during some downtime when we both have time to focus and be present. I am looking forward to chatting with you.

Remember:

- Communication spans beyond verbal. Be sensitive to your gestures and facial expressions.
- Allow the person a sacred space to also speak. They may have additional things they are ready to discuss, since your initial conversation. Everyone has had a chance to pause and think a bit more.
- Try to be open, honest, and resist being defensive or attacking. This is a conversation.
- Check your ego at the door. This is not about being right. Remember your goals and what you will do, in the event you become emotional or off-centered

Stop 16: Affirmation Alley

AFFIRMATION

Affirmations are gifts to you from you, one of the greatest you'll ever receive

Far from conceit, these words possess power and are truths you must believe

For whether you possess them now or it is a future revelation to come true

Insist on speaking your affirmation daily, for it's a gift I offer to you

Remember you are strength, you are power, and you are worthy of the greatness that lies ahead

My message is to avoid distractions and focus on declaring your value instead

Articulate your strengths, those you have and those you aspire to achieve

Trust what others say you do well, as it's oftentimes difficult to perceive

"**I** am" are the words to speak aloud, with your strength tacked to the end

Offer this gift to others, as they affirm what they may not yet know

Nourish your mind with positive declarations and your confidence will begin to show

Welcome to Affirmation Alley!

THE STOP: THE AFFIRMATION

Affirmations are declarations that verify your greatness. This stop offers gifts to you, from you. Grab hold and treasure this powerful and personal gift for exactly what it is. As affirmations are repeated, they assert positive energy into your mind, body, and soul. They transmit to your brain and drive actions that align with what you now know to be true.

MY STORY: MY AFFIRMATION

After dropping him off for school and turning off the light that somehow remained on in his bedroom, I found myself on the floor in front of the Ikea mirror that leaned against the Avengers-themed wall, in his private super-hero haven. Through tears, I spoke aloud to God and wondered how I got to this place of sadness, with feelings of non-progression. Still sobbing, I began professing aloud what I was grateful for, and what blessings I had flowing in my direction. I talked about the tough times that seemed to weigh heavier each day. For each trial I spoke aloud, I forced myself to talk about the good that was also within it, the lessons I learned, and what I was grateful for within each circumstance.

As I occasionally took deep breaths, through my bent-over stature that resembled a fetus in the womb, I could feel a calm physically passing over my entire body. I was amazed at the energy I could feel and the release that was physically happening. I pulled myself to sit straight and began affirming my strengths in the mirror. After a prayer of thanks and a long hot shower, I wrote down what I recalled from the affirmation that had brought me so much peace. Would I believe what I affirmed to myself? Could I shift from the limiting thoughts of my present circumstance to see the good that was right before me? Could these affirmations help me maintain the calm that had come over me? Could they become part of my routine to give thanks and command intention each morning?

YOUR STORY: YOUR AFFIRMATION

There is so much power in affirming your strengths and who you are destined to be.

Grab 3 of the strengths you wrote at Stop 4: Strength Street. Write them here beside each I AM.

I am

____

I am

____

I am

____

I am

____

(insert your first, middle, and last name)

Now read the collective "I am's" together in front of a mirror. This is YOUR affirmation.

How does that make you feel?

____

How else does it make you feel?

____

____

____

____

Here's a message from me to you.

You are worthy. You are more than enough. You are each of the strengths listed above.

When you affirm who you are, you are giving thanks for all you have. As we journey to our next stop, Gratitude Gateway, this feeling of calmness will continue to permeate your being.

Stop 17: Gratitude Gateway

GRATITUDE

Gratitude is the gateway that offers thanks for what you have and for what you don't

Relish in appreciation of what others simply won't

A power beyond yourself has helped you navigate the road you're on today

Trust your strengths, faith, and instincts to grant you guidance on your way

Insist on appreciation words like "thank you," as you move your ego to the side

Track your small wins daily because from these you'll not want to hide

Unique to you, these small wins become large victories over time

Dare to embrace each situation as a footstool that helps you climb

Execute with excellence and allow your light to shine

Welcome to Gratitude Gateway!

THE STOP: THE GRATITUDE

The gateway to gratitude is your gateway to happiness. It opens a passageway that allows you to give thanks and to also appreciate all you've been blessed with, no matter how great or small. Gratitude allows you to give of yourself to help others. It helps you recognize that you did not get to this place on your own. The power that I regard as my God, or your spiritual guide, family, friends and/or others, have helped you along your journey. Gratitude is showing gratefulness and thankfulness, even in the midst of any circumstance.

MY STORY: MY GRATITUDE

"Say Yes & Thank You!" my cousins reminded me at the dining room table immediately after my Visioning & Beyond VIP Workshop that I had facilitated for 25 women. As we reviewed my vision board and talked of all its components, they reminded me of two key aspects to consider adding to the images and words already assembled. They suggested the phrases "Say Yes" and "Thank You." While I remind clients of this daily, it is oftentimes your family or strong support who will remind you, by telling it to you how you need to hear it, straight with no chaser! They advised me that I was blocking my blessings if I did not add these affirmations to the vision of where I wanted to go and how I would get there. Just like that and in that moment, one of my boy-wonder cousins reached into his pocket and invested cash into Walker & Walker Enterprises.

Could I avoid my typical "no thank you," or "don't worry about it" and simply be grateful in the moment? Would I allow myself to receive by saying "Yes" and "Thank You?" Could I appreciate their coaching and be grateful that my family was gathered right here to support me? Would I carry on what was added to my vision board throughout the year to receive, appreciate, and honor what I had right before me?

YOUR STORY: YOUR GRATITUDE

What are you grateful for? Consider turning your list into a board of "small wins & gratitude" where you add a line each day. In my instance, I would write:

Today's Date	Small Wins & Gratitude *By Lolita*	Small Wins & Gratitude *By Insert Name*
3/26/18	**Win:** Accepting a cash investment for W&WE **Grateful:** Family reminder of "yes" and "thank you"	

Now is your time to Embrace, to Act, and to Thrive. You deserve every blessing coming your way! Own it.

Here's a few thoughts that have worked for me and I would love to pass them along to you.

- Vision where you want to go and shout it from the mountaintops. Place that vision, using images, phrases, and words within a prominent location, where you can see it and reflect each day.
- Communicate your vision, though it can be a bit scary, to share your dreams and instantly feel a sense of accountability.
- Affirm yourself daily to set intention for your day.

- Create a routine that allows you to incorporate your gratitude and small wins daily.

I have found this daily routine shifts your mindset, your approach to life, and the results of your day.

Consider making your Small Win & Gratitude Board a part of your daily routine by including the names of your family members across the top row, granting everyone their own space. Consider trying it before or after dinner to allow gratitude gateway into family conversations and communications. Have fun!

THE ENDING

Well, we've returned to the station and are now concluding your journey aboard Lolita's Change Train. Thanks for hopping aboard.

Writing this book has been an experience of self-discovery and growth. Oftentimes, through laughs, tears, recollections, and deep conversations with myself, I have managed to pull some of the emotions that resulted from changes I have experienced throughout my life. The journey has, of course, been therapeutic, eye opening, humbling, and an emotional roller coaster, to put it mildly.

Sometimes you don't quite realize just how big of a leap you have taken when you are grounded in the affirmation that you are already enough. My leap from everything I knew in Corporate America pushed me to start a new business without hesitation, host my first major event, a sold-out women's retreat, in only seven months, facilitate workshops, write a book, empower women to thrive, journey with my mom through her survival of breast cancer, and simply rediscover myself, to name a few. How did I do it? Simply by focusing on the pieces I could own and not what was outside my sphere of control. The journey has been quite remarkable. I still tear up as I read certain parts of my story, however, it is par for the course. There is such beauty that lies within it. I am blessed to have been able to share my stories and have high hopes that they have helped you craft your own.

What is my further hope for you? I hope that while you were aboard Lolita's Change Train, that each of the seventeen stops offered you nuggets of yourself that you had not yet tapped into. I hope you have rediscovered or discovered new strengths that now have the space to surface. I hope you remember that to affirm you is to believe in you, and to believe in you is to know that you are greater than where you stand today. **Thanks for trusting me on your journey and congratulations for leaping into the greatness that was awaiting you.** You still have so much to discover. This is only your new beginning.

Thank you

APPENDICES

APPENDIX A

The transition bridge of change

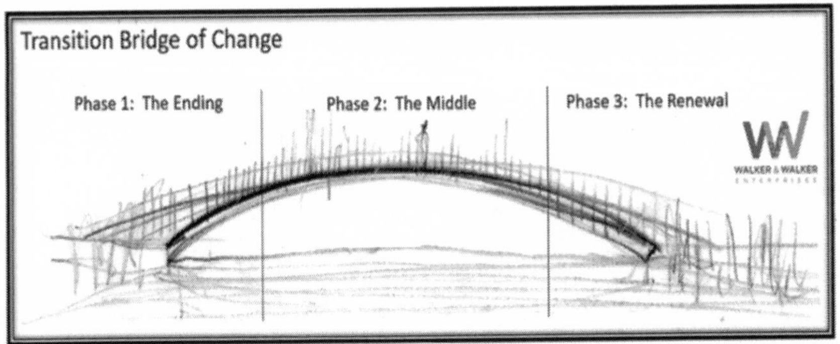

APPENDIX B

The Grid for the Transition Bridge of Change

	Phase 1: The Ending	Phase 2: The Middle	Phase 3: The Renewal
The Feelings	Sadness, loss, denial, frustration, them-vs-us mentality, anger	Resentment, confusion, anxiety, impatience, skepticism	Excitement, acceptance, commitment, energy, openness to new beginnings
The Realities	You must accept the ending of something to then accept the newness of another. This is not always easy. The focus on what you can control is helpful in this phase.	You may feel that chaos is all around and that you are always busy. You may be taking on more, see lower morale, or gaps in your normal productivity. Surprisingly, creativity and innovative ways of thinking may be sparked.	You are seeing and feeling a new and revived energy from those who are now embracing change alongside you. You are able to highlight big and small wins of success and results.
The Reminders	Settling in this phase for an extended period may force you to be left behind. It can also mean those who depend on you could adopt your mindset, then struggle with moving to the next phase.	You and/or some who are on the change journey with you, may still be attached to old thinking and methods. You and they may, therefore need help in which direction, backward or forward, to travel.	You are seeing what a new beginning looks and feels like. Embrace the newness of change that has come to be your normal. While you are still adjusting, you are allowing yourself to thrive. Use your wins to help others who are still in Phase 1 and 2 to progress toward Phase 3.

APPENDIX C

The Small Wins & Gratitude Board

Today's Date	Small Wins & Gratitude *By Lolita*	Small Wins & Gratitude *By Insert Name*
3/26/18	**Win:** Accepting a cash investment for W&WE **Grateful:** Family reminder of "yes" and "thank you"	

APPENDIX D

The Walker & Walker Enterprises BE FREE Creed

Believe in your strengths & open your mind to now explore
Expect moments to have meanings, which propel you to soar
Face your fears head on, yet hold them at bay
Release what is not progressing you on today
Experience the unexpected, what you would normally let pass by
Embrace the renewed you, who is now free to fly

Empowering YOU to embrace, act, & thrive in change

THE DISCOVERIES, NOTES, & RECOLLECTIONS

Your whitespace, Your Thoughts

THE DISCOVERIES, NOTES, & RECOLLECTIONS

Your whitespace, Your Thoughts

THE DISCOVERIES, NOTES, & RECOLLECTIONS

Your whitespace, Your Thoughts

THE DISCOVERIES, NOTES, & RECOLLECTIONS

Your whitespace, Your Thoughts

THE DISCOVERIES, NOTES, & RECOLLECTIONS

Your whitespace, Your Thoughts

THE AUTHOR

Lolita Emanuelle Walker is a mother, certified life and executive coach, change champion, and a lover of all things that makes her smile.

Alongside her coaching and consultancy, Lolita facilitates annual women's renewal retreats, bringing together busy women to pause, reflect, re-discover, and renew. (www.lolitawalker.com)

Though she does work with male clients both through coaching and organizational work, her passion truly resides in the empowerment of women, who in her mind, are caregivers who oftentimes forget to care for themselves. In the sentiments of a longtime client, "these words are her retreat in a book." From retreats, to coaching, speaking, and writing personalized affirmations for others, to name a few, Lolita does "all-things-empowerment."

She finds passion in enabling others to tap into themselves and pull the greatness that lies within. She knows and appreciates that you are power, you are passion, and you have a purpose.

It is this affirmation that serves as the platform to which you will stand upon when you are ready to journey aboard Lolita's Change Train.

Lolita graduated from Morgan State University as an Industrial Engineer and Simmons College as an MBA. An active member of Alpha Kappa Alpha Sorority, Incorporated and several volunteer organizations, she is a sole proprietor who has lived, experienced and thrived in both transition and change. Her background and passion have fueled her approach for others to be free, believe, trust, and renew. Ms. Walker is a motivator, an empowerment rockstar, and a change champion for you.

Connect with her at info@lolitawalker.com or www.lolitawalker.com.

THE BEHIND THE BOOK

When I am asked about why I chose to write a book now versus earlier or later in my life, I simply reply, "because now is the perfect time in my journey." I firmly believe that God puts us in spaces and places for a reason and in our own season. At this point in my life, I am 40 years old and I am set on living my best life. As I journey, I move forward knowing I have so many wins that I have achieved along the way. I am fabulous, fierce, and fun. I have a vision that is guiding me. I will continue to push myself as I prepare to further soar and will ask others to do the same as they travel with me. I am proud of me. I am proud that my experiences have shaped me into the person I am today.

This book is my time to share my passion and stories with the world.

I am passionate about helping women thrive. Taking on burdens that are not our own and getting in our own way will handcuff the essentials of life. We must breathe, recollect ourselves, and push forward with clarity. This is something that instinctively happens. It is work and it is deliberate.

The title "The Intersection of You & Change" resulted from an image I saw as I wrote the different chapters within this book. Through each stop, I could see myself standing at an intersection. I, then began thinking of all the decisions and experiences in my life, some of which I shared within this book, some I share as I engage with others, and some I have yet to reveal. Despite if you are on a journey with others or riding solo, the decisions to be made throughout your journey are personal and ultimately reside with you.

THE BONUS BOOK

Thanks again for reading my first book, *The Intersection of You & Change.* Please check out an excerpt from my next book, which is a shift in thinking from my last. It is targeted to men, women, boys, and girls, who are interested in learning, appreciating, and embracing affirmations. Here we go!

It was the 1960's and the first year of integration at Forest Glen High School in Suffolk Virginia. She was one of only eleven African American students who were being bussed in. Against her own desires, her mother knew she would be part of the history to ensure there was equal education for all. "We were no less than anyone else. We were powerful, we were strong, we were phenomenal, we were worthy. We deserved every bit of everything that anyone had on this earth." These were the professions of her mom. Though being taught these lessons at home, my mother and her cousin would become juniors in a new high school, with the world weighing upon their shoulders and eyes gazing upon their faces. They each housed numerous feelings of anxiety, inferiority, panic, insecurity, and fear, which rose quickly as each day reached closer and the bus finally pulled up. They also had a sense of pride, convinced that this opportunity afforded them a better quality of education, one that they deserved.

I am Lolita E. Walker and I am 4 generations removed from slavery. My 87-year old grandmother reminded me that the road has already been paved for each of us. "Love it, appreciate it, embrace it." She engrained that my ancestors have worked too hard, my family has sacrificed too much, and there are too many others who have endured ups and downs to build the foundation to which I stand on today. "NOW IS YOUR TIME!" she repeated while staring in my eyes.

This book is a collection of personal, powerful, and poetic affirmations. You will read those I have written for men, women, boys, and girls, and those I have created just for your coffee table. Use it for chats with friends, family, and even reflections of your own. Envision your life, your energy, your situation now and how you want to live it in the future. Use each affirmation as a platform for book clubs and groups. Own these affirmations, declare them, and live them! You are stronger because of where you have been. It is time to affirm where you are going. Have fun on your journey of commitment, laughter, fun, and affirmations. Thanks for allowing me to be a part of it.

"the ceo"

I wrote this affirmation for a CEO I met for the first time, while chatting at a bar one night. This affirmation reminds us that we are all human, no matter the position. We are all vulnerable and at some point, await the affirmation that we are enough, as we transition into different phases of our journey. As this gentleman spoke, I knew that the power of a personal affirmation would increase his confidence and allow him to be more effective as a strategic thinker and a leader that his employees would follow. He had risen from ranks within the company and was now a power player deserving of his seat, not only at the executive table, but leading the members that sat around HIS executive table. A reminder was overdue.

I am *exactly where I want AND where I need to be*

I am *worthy of unleashing the powerful CEO in me*

I am *confident, I am experienced, I am open to the lessons afforded to me each day*

I am *committed to speaking power words that move me out of my own way*

I am *THE owner, THE strategic decision maker, THE leader in my space*

I am *driven to propel my business because I am who sets the pace*

I am *power, I am focused, I am ENOUGH right here and right now*

I am *walking as a determined Powerhouse who will show the industry how*

I am *an affirmer of and for my people, I am in touch with their work and their needs of me*

I am *the voice, I am the pinnacle, I am the direction-setter they trust and see*

…………………………

For your own personalized, powerful and poetic "Affirmation by Lolita," please contact info@lolitawalker.com.

Please stay connected at www.lolitawalker.com .